MAAA!

Why Hearing God's Voice is Essential to Motherhood

MAAA!

Why Hearing God's Voice is Essential to Motherhood

Evangelist Angie BEE

LADERO INSPIRATION published by
Ladero Press LLC
229 Kettering Road
Deltona, Florida 32725

First Ladero Press Printing, October 2018

MAAA!: Why Hearing God's Voice is Essential to Motherhood
Copyright © 2018 by Angela Neal
All rights reserved.
ISBN: 978-1-946981-14-1 Paperback / 978-1-946981-16-5 Mobi / 978-1-946981-17-2 Epub
Printed in the United States of America
Set in Palatino Linotype
Cover Designed by Adam Holt, Angela Neal, and LaShalonda Robinson

Scripture quotations are taken from the Holy Bible, New Living Translation, Copyright ©1996, 2004, 2007, 2013, 2015 by Tyndale House Foundation. Used by permission of Tyndale House Publishers, Inc., Carol Stream, Illinois 60188. All rights reserved.

Scripture quotations are taken from The Holy Bible, King James Version. Cambridge Edition: 1769; King James Bible Online, 2018. www.kingjamesbibleonline.org.

Scriptures taken from the Holy Bible, New International Version®, NIV®. Copyright © 1973, 1978, 1984, 2011 by Biblica, Inc.™ Used by permission of Zondervan. All rights reserved worldwide. www.zondervan.com The "NIV" and "New International Version" are trademarks registered in the United States Patent and Trademark Office by Biblica, Inc.™

Lines from Mahogany quoted under fair use copyright provisions.

All rights reserved. The reproduction, transmission, or utilization of this work in whole or in part in any form by any electronic, mechanical or other means, now known or hereafter invented, including xerography, photocopying and recording, or in any information storage or retrieval system, is forbidden without written permission. For permission, please contact Ladero Press Editors at editors@laderopress.com.

Library of Congress information available upon request.
www.laderopress.com

*Dedicated to the women,
mothers, daughters and young ladies in my life.
My family and ministry are built upon our
interactions, and I am grateful that
God placed you in my life.*

Contents

Foreword vii

World War II 1

Saying Goodbye to Her Mother 7

Asking Your Children For Help 10

Trying To Raise A Grown Child 14

Boys Vs. Girls 17

Learning From Other Moms 20

After You're Gone 23

Use That Cash-Money 26

The Time Is Now 1:38 30

    "Where Are You Staying?" 35

    "Why Are You Here?" 39

    "What Time is it?" 43

Foreword

When asked if I would write the foreword for The Queen Bee: Ms Angie BEE! I was honored to do so, simply because when I put out the call for guest bloggers for #SpiritualSundays, she was the very first to respond! That's what spiritual sisters do-- they show up and show out! Kinda reminds me of someone else--our Heavenly Father! Isn't He the greatest?

As you turn the pages of this book, you will not be disappointed! Ms. Angie Bee will take you on a roller coaster ride of your life with the stories that she shares about motherhood. Buckle up, hold on tight, and oh yeah, enjoy the ride!

Tamara D McCarthy

a.k.a, *Single Mom of Purpose*

World War II

I recently learned that at one time in our history, there were several city streets in the United States of America that became littered with propaganda posters. The posters read, "Loose Lips Sink Ships!" The term was originally intended to caution a person away from excessive talking; for fear that what they were saying may cause the demise of a plan if the wrong person heard it!

Someone should have explained that reasoning about excessive talking to my eldest daughter. She can say "Maaa!" with the best of them.

Please do not get me wrong! My daughter is a delightful young woman and was a blessing to have in my daily life as she was growing up. She has a "bubbly" type of personality; the light in the room brightens when she enters, and she is the friend that everyone likes to be with. You can hear her laugh from a mile away and she can tell a story like no other! I would enjoy having her as a radio show host because with that excessive talking of hers, there would never be a lapse in the show! She definitely is my child, as she learned this excessive talking trait from me, and I learned it from MY mother.

What did you learn from YOUR mother? What did you inherit from your mother or her mother or a "mothering-type" that was in your life? Do you share this information with others? That is the way we begin our group discussions at each "Moms-n-Ministry" workshop; we share the knowledge and wisdom that was instilled in us that makes our villages strong.

The Moms-n-Ministry workshop was founded in January 2013 and included three eclectic mothers sharing their testimonies, books, expertise, and their blessings. Attendees were engaged, entertained, and enthralled, and the videos that we played during the workshop truly hit the point! Now the Moms-n-Ministry workshop continues to travel sharing the gospel of Jesus Christ, as only a mom can do and that workshop is just one of the inspirations behind this book. Get ready to glean, reminisce, share, and give God the praise through it all!

I grew up in Detroit Michigan with my mom, dad, a poodle, some gerbils, and two younger sisters that just so happened to be twins. Tanya and Sonya came home from the hospital to my loving and welcoming 5-year-old arms! I could not have been more delighted as there was one baby for my mom to play with and one baby for ME to play with. Nothing else mattered to me in life at that time because I was the BIG sister! I could hold the baby and give her a bottle. I could hand the safety pins to my mom when changing their cloth diapers, and I was the only one that could interpret their baby talk. Life was good, and I enjoyed my days. Never in my wildest dreams would I have understood the challenges that my mom faced having three pre-school aged girls to raise, while my dad worked swing shifts at Chrysler.

Decades later, I found myself reminiscing with my mother's best friend. My mom's life ended in November 1999, and as I talk with her friends, an entirely different aspect of my mother is revealed. "You know, your mom called me one summer day in tears. She was actually thinking about holding you back from starting kindergarten because you were such a big help to her with the twins," mom's friend stated. "Really?" I replied. "What did you say to her?" I asked. "I told her that it was her responsibility to let you go and grow and learn. She couldn't keep you from growing up, and she would find other ways to handle the twins – on her own." In addition, with that, I learned my first lesson on motherhood.

What did you learn from your mom that you would want to pass along to a new mother?

_____

_____

_____

What did you learn from your mother's friend that made you look at your mother differently?

_____

_____

_____

As I was attempting to raise my own daughters, I would reflect on the ways my mother raised my sisters and me, and I was determined to do a better job! You see, when my mother was angry, I would get "the belt." When I did something in a different way that my mother would have expected me to do it, I would get "the belt." If I looked at mom the wrong way, here comes "the belt." I did not know a thing about "spare the rod and spoil the child;" all I knew was that belt would be the death of me with all those raised whelps and cuts on my arms and legs.

I refused to spank my daughters with a belt while I was raising them and opted for a "stern talking" as a form of correction. "Let's not do this" "I don't want you to do that" "How do you feel about this or that?" I would ask. What I learned from my mother was that there were other ways to raise a child. As a result, my daughters are no more or less than my sisters and I, yet the accomplishment that I feel when I reflect on raising them is something indescribable.

Do you feel a sense of accomplishment and joy when you see the "fruits of your labor?" The turmoil that I experienced as a child and a teen was comparable to a war where two factions were trying to defeat one another. My mom was trying to raise me as best she could, and I was trying to figure out my own way of doing things. The result of World War II is that city streets were littered with propaganda, encouraging secrets to be kept and information not to be shared. After the death of my mother, I truly missed her guidance. How was I supposed to raise my daughters without my mom? This is where I learned to look to God.

I will lift up mine eyes unto the hills, from whence cometh my help. (Psalm 121:1 KJV).

My help comes from the LORD, the Maker of heaven and earth (Psalm 121:2 NIV).

I answered the phone this morning, and my youngest was in the midst of a full-blown anxiety attack while at work.

"Mom, I'm freaking out!" she exclaimed! After asking her a few questions to be sure she was in a safe place, I decided to drive the ninety minutes to her city to see her. Sometimes, a mom just has to "see" her kid to calm her OWN nerves.

Praying all the way to her office, I reflected upon the last major anxiety attack I had while on the job. That attack resulted in my loss of unemployment benefits because I had "walked off the job" and had failed to speak to a supervisor. After years of learning to manage symptoms through prayer, medication, counseling, and family support... now I am headed down the road to show my baby some support. I sure hope I can help!

Saying Goodbye to Her Mother

While growing up in Detroit, I attended Fredrick J. Schulze Elementary School. All I can remember are wonderful experiences while a student there. In the third grade, I became friends with another student that is now named "Lei." She lived less than a mile from my home, and over the years, we would ride our bicycles together and spend time chatting on the phone together.

During my college years, I relocated to Florida where I pursued careers and married. After my divorce, I chose to raise my daughters away from my entire family, who lived in Michigan. My mom would often call me and say, "Guess who I ran into at the credit union today?" Even though I knew what her response would be, I would reply, "Who did you see, Ma?" And she would reply, "Your old friend Lisa. The one that changed her name to Lei!" Evidentially, they both shared the same payday and would bump into each other and catch up, and I would then be privileged to the details of their conversation. Lei and I never really "talked" to each other during those years, but we surely kept in touch through that regular meeting at the credit union.

In the fall of 1999 when my mother died, I ran into Lei at church. When I told her that I was returning to Detroit to be closer to my family, she welcomed me home with loving arms. She was now serving as a Girl Scout troupe leader, and my daughters joined her troupe! She was an extra pair of mothering "eyes" that I appreciated during that time of grief, and I will always be grateful to God for her. Our families would gather for fellowship dinner on Saturday nights, playing Spades and sharing memories, and our kids had the opportunity to hear our stories. This young mother, who started out as my third-grade classmate, was now serving as a mother to me, helping guide me towards a new life, without my mother.

Lei's mom transitioned to heaven in April 2017, and I was in Detroit to be with her. My friend is now a grandmother, and her children were all in the family home with her, but there is nothing like having a house full of love when you have suffered a loss.

My sister accompanied me to Lei's home, and she witnessed our interaction and was entrenched in our brief reflections of our mothers. Lei had been her mother's primary caregiver for more than a decade, and now, my prayers for my friend include requesting that God fill those potentially empty spaces in her now vacated life.

I composed the following reflection for the funeral of Lei's mother... and now I share my words with each of you.

The first time I met mother, she was sitting at the kitchen table and greeted me with a curious smile. I later suspected that the look of correction that she gave me was because of my loud, boisterous laughter upon entering her home! She was a quiet mother in my life, and I loved her daughter Lei.

Sometimes, I would ride my bike over to the house to see if Lei could come out to play, and mother would greet me at the door. She always seemed to just gently smile at me as if to say, "Here she comes again!" She always invited me in, always offered to feed me, and she always let me spend time with my best friend.

Over the years as her health declined, I admired mother's spirit as it glowed through her grandchildren. Watching them grow into adults has been a true testimony to mother. When I entered her bedroom last summer, during my visit to Detroit, those expressive and loving eyes again greeted me. It does my heart good to know that she is at her peaceful Heavenly home now, and I am honored to have been blessed by her smile.

Asking Your Children For Help

For some strange reason, some mothers seem to feel as if they cannot ask their children for help or advice. Consider the mother of a toddler that feeds, clothes, bathes, and teaches her child. Does that mother ask the child to wash the dishes or take out the trash? I do not think so. What about the mother of a teen? Is that teen ever asked to get a job to support the family or pay the mortgage? How about elderly mothers that struggle to live in a home alone; do they ask their children to pay their bills, care for their physical needs, or place them in assisted living? Not really. Some mothers strive to accomplish most things on their own without asking their children for help until there comes such a time when they receive godly wisdom, or an epiphany comes their way.

When my youngest child was a teen, the symptoms of major depression hit me with a vengeance! Not only did my daughter learn to cook by herself, but she also learned which utility bills needed to be paid, how to pay them, and how to ask for a payment arrangement. She began to recognize my symptoms and guide me in managing them. She even learned how to count my pills, gently encouraged me to bathe, and helped me as I learned to live again. Only an anointing from Our Father could have guided Jasmine along this path, and I truly believe God has a path for her to walk in this life.

Now, years later, those symptoms crept up on me again. Have you ever looked at yourself in a picture and saw that you have gained weight? *Where did those fluffy cheeks come from? Who put that belly on me?* The symptoms crept up on me like added pounds, and I could not remember if I had faced them in the past. I never kept a journal of my healing (although I really need to do that!), and I truly did not want to return to the doctor's office and face hospitalization, so I called my youngest for help.

Jasmine reminded me that these current symptoms were some of the same ones I had faced earlier. I was grateful for her help. She continued to bless me by also reminding me of something even more important – I was advised not to remain on my current cocktail of antidepressants for more than 7-8 years due to the decrease in effectiveness; that was more than ten years ago. "Mom, it's time to try something new!" Thank you, God, for speaking to me through my child.

A couple of years ago, my mother's best friend and I sat down for a talk. My mom died suddenly in 1999 and left my sisters and me with several truly wonderful women that are lovely, wise, and strong. During a conversation with the lovely green-eyed friend, she told me a story that touched my heart.

Earlier, I told you that I have twin sisters and how thrilled I remember being about their arrival! I passed my mom the giant safety pins she needed when she changed their diapers (cloth diapers in the 70s – ya'll don't know anything about that!)

Taking care of my babies is probably one of my first childhood memories, yet my mother's friend remembers it differently. She told me that my mother called her in tears one day as she grappled with the fact that I would be entering kindergarten soon. "Who is going to help me with these babies?" my mom asked her friend. "Do you think I could keep her out of school until next year?" my mom pleaded.

Of course, I had no memory of being a helper to my mom as I was just having fun. According to Madame Green-Eyes, my mom saw things differently. With my dad working odd shifts and rarely being hands-on, and with a new house to care for along with two infants and an overactive preschooler to control, mom was searching for help! As she reached out to her friend for advice, she conceded that her plan would have set me back in my educational process. I believe it was at that moment that mom came to the unfortunate false realization that she could not ask her child for help.

Some widows are homebound because they do not want to "burden" their children or ask them for help.

Aged fathers are trying to cook meals or manage lawn care because they do not want to disturb the lives of their grown children.

Parents die unexpectedly, having succumbed to un-medicated symptoms because they did not want to "worry" their children or ask for their help purchasing medication.

Now, their children no longer have that dad or that mom in their lives.

The Bible teaches us in Psalm 121:2 (NLT) *"My help comes from the LORD, who made heaven and earth!"* Moms, please recognize that the Holy Spirit should lead your every waking moment, especially when you are raising your children. Do not make a move until you seek the Lord! Also, recognize that Our Father has sent us help in our day-to-day lives, and sometimes, that help may need to come from our children. I erroneously believed that I was stifling my daughter from enjoying her teen years because she had to manage our bills and prepare meals; for years, I carried that guilt. Now that I see her as a young adult managing her finances, setting and achieving financial goals, I realize that she received the help that she needed during those times. Our help comes from the Lord! Ask your children for their help, and watch the Lord raise them up during that time, and at a later time, as well.

Have you ever asked your child for advice or for assistance? Why or why not? As you now reflect upon aspects of your life, in which ways could your child have assisted you if you had only asked?

_____

_____

_____

Trying To Raise A Grown Child

I saw a Facebook post today that urged men and women of God to stop gossiping about a person's shortcoming and speak up when something is not correct in a person's life. My mind immediately went to my children. When you raise emotional daughters and they remain sensitive as young adults, sometimes you tiptoe around issues.

Take, for example, my friend who is a single parent. She was determined to raise her daughter in the ways of the Lord, take her to church, and share scriptures with her. She taught her daughter the importance of tithes and offerings and exposed her to ministry outreach and fellowship. When this single mother's daughter became pregnant out-of-wedlock, she "washed her hands" of the situation and opted to let her grown child raise herself in this situation.

Our kids turn 18 years old and in the United States, they are considered adults. However, does that mean that we stop "raising" them? Statistics show that more twenty-something- and thirty-something-year-old children are moving back home with their parents, and in most cases, they return home with their children.

On my thirtieth birthday, I found myself at my mother's kitchen table, blowing out candles on a homemade birthday cake created by my two pre-school daughters. The three of us were living with my mom as I recovered from injuries sustained in a car accident and as I waited for my final divorce papers to arrive. Yes, I was living with my mom, and I thought that she was helping me raise my daughters, but what I now know is that she was continuing to raise me! It was at that time that my mother began to inform me of medical conditions in our family that she thought I should be aware of. I had already begun to lose my hair and was secretly trying to deal with it.

My mother taught me about the alopecia that she was diagnosed with and helped me address some lifestyle options. Mom raised me to accept that as I was healing from my injuries, I may need to teach my children how to become a bit more independent and learn to help one another. My daughters are only two years apart in age, yet they remind me so much of my twin sisters that I sometimes forget that they ARE NOT twins! Mom raised me to see the differences in their personalities and how those differences would allow them to have different skill sets in life. My mom raised me to be able to raise my children.

How did your mom raise you? Did she lead by example or was she more hands-on with you?

When you "think back over your life," how do you view your mom's training methods? Are there aspects of how she raised you that you feel that you will NEVER repeat while raising your children? Do you feel that you want to raise your children in the same manner that your mother/motherly-type raised you? Do you rejoice and give God praise for the lessons that you learned from your mom? Do you acknowledge your mom and thank her on occasions other than Mother's Day?

The Bible actually gives us two separate translations of children acknowledging their mothers. If you Google the scripture Proverbs 31:28, you will see that the New International Version states, *Her children arise and call her blessed,* while the New Living Translation states, *Her children stand and bless her.* Praise God; my children have done both! My daughters have reminded me of the blessings they have witnessed in my life, and they have blessed me (indeed) by the way they have grown to respect the lives and situations that God has granted them.

Now, in my quest to try and raise a GROWN child, I realize that scolding and "time-outs" are not what they need. Grown children need prayer, wisdom, and support. However, we parents need to understand that our children may know the pitfalls that we taught them; yet, they will sometimes have to drag themselves out of their own pits in order to learn to reach up for God instead of reaching up for us Steering them in the direction of God Almighty is the best way to raise an adult child!

Boys Vs. Girls

– WHAT'S A MOM TO DO?

Mothers with sons raise them differently than mothers with daughters do. This was a statement embedded in me by my mom. Since I had no brothers, uncles or male cousins in my life regularly, I became fascinated by that statement! *What was my mother telling me that was different from what another mother was telling her son?* I wondered.

As a teenager, I recognized that boys were asked to do different types of chores around the house and that boys were allowed to do more "outdoor activities" than girls. Girls took sewing classes while boys took up football or basketball. Girls were taught to raise a family while boys were taught to finance the family. Girls were taught to "keep our legs closed" while boys were taught to "sow their wild oats."

Later in life, I learned that mothers with daughters raised them to care for their own children while mothers of sons raised them to one-day return and care for them. It was always understood that women outlived their husbands and would then rely on their sons to care for them.

Interestingly enough – that lesson was learned from the Bible!

In the book of Ruth, Chapters 1-4, we learn of a mother named Naomi whose husband and sons were all killed. The sons had married women, so Naomi was left with no means to care for herself or her daughters-in-law.

A house full of childless widows! The chapter shows us that it was the culture for a mother to be cared for by her sons after the death of her husband, so Naomi was in dire straits now that all the men in her life were gone. I see now why my eighty-eight-year-old grandmother calls my father EVERY MORNING to check on him, and how he now uses the key to her home to pop over and check on her. Yes, my aunt does a wonderful job caring for my grandmother, but there is something different about the expectations that grandma has of my father to care for her now that she is of a certain age. Hmmmm.

I was a mother that raised daughters, and I married a man that raised sons. One of the first things I asked my then-fiancé as we were conversing one day is, "How do you teach your sons how they should treat a lady?" Bartee's response was simple, "I teach them by showing how I treat their mother."

Often, young ladies are taught to watch how a man treats his mother, and that is a good indicator as to how he will treat them. However, what happens when you aren't able to witness these interactions? What is a good indicator? How do you teach your daughters to look out for scoundrels, and how do you teach your sons to respect young ladies, and not fall for the okie-doke? Does a mother truly need a man in order to raise her son? Does a father need a woman around to raise his daughter? Can single parents successfully co-parent without being in a relationship with one another? How can grandparents raise their grandchildren without the interaction of a male or female "parent role-model" in that child's life?

Hmmm.

Learning From Other Moms
SINCE OUR FIRST MOMS-N-MINISTRY WORKSHOP JANUARY 2013

Mothers have been quite expressive with their thoughts, opinions, and wisdom. Some of the most memorable bits of love we have recorded from past sessions are:

- Put a pot of beans on the stove in the morning and by dinnertime, you will not have to cook.

- Save your leftovers from the week and make a casserole with it to store in the freezer.

- Do all of your laundry on Friday night so you can enjoy your weekend.

- Always have a side hustle or side business in addition to your job. You need more income just to finance a child's education and school expenses.

- Watch TV with your kids, and do not use TV as a babysitter.

- Play video games with your kids, and do not allow them to stay in their room for hours, withdrawn from the rest of the family.

- Take bullying seriously! Don't just go up to the school but teach your child coping skills.

- Teach your kids how to catch the bus, how to learn and read street signs, and how to save money to catch a cab/Uber. They need to know how to get home.

- Prepare your meals in anticipation for the family to dine together, at least once a day. Do not let your kids skip breakfast. Eat with them! Meet them at school once a month, eat lunch with them, and expect the family to enjoy dinner together without the TV!

Now, you have done all you can to put your kids on a proper path of life, and still they find ways to become sexually active; they still choose to "vape" and smoke marijuana; and they still choose to become the neighborhood drug dealer. What do you do? How do you address their behavior without nagging? Do you call the police on your child? It is bad enough when your co-worker has bad breath or you find your neighbor stealing from your water hose, but how do you tell your child that you are disappointed in them and you want their behavior to change? Proverbs 22:6 teaches us to "Train up a child in the way he should go; even when he is old he will not depart from it." You took your child to Bible study, Sunday service, Vacation Bible School, and you spanked your child frequently. Yet, she still ended up working in the strip club, and he still had three baby-mamas with no means of paying child support. Your child has departed from their teaching, and you do not know what to do!

Maaa! Have you cried out to the Lord for direction? Have you asked advice from Mother Johnson over at the church? What about your auntie or the neighbor down the street? Godly wisdom is not going to fall out the sky on your head; you have to seek it, accept it, and apply it!

What advice did you receive from an older woman in your life that helped you raise your child?

_____

_____

_____

What advice would you share with a younger mother as they raise their children?

_____

_____

_____

After You're Gone

Recently, my daughter came over for a visit, and while we were having breakfast, she asked me a question that inspired this chapter.

"Mom, you are always behind the video camera. How am I going to 'see' you after you're gone?"

My response, "You mean, after I am dead?"

"Yes, mom! While eating my blueberry pancakes, I'm asking you how I can remember you after you are DEAD!" she belligerently responded.

"Well, I've got YouTube videos!"

"Maaa! I don't want to see videos of you that the world sees; I want to see something special for ME!"

Well, that really got me thinking. What do we leave our children as a legacy of our love for them? Generations of families have passed down recipes in cookbooks, and each time that recipe is prepared, it brings a joyful reminder to the taste buds. My mom left us a recipe for her Holiday Cockroach Cake (inside family joke... ask me the ingredients when you meet me in person!)

Proverbs 13:22 (KJV) teaches us, *A good man leaveth an*

inheritance to his children's children. I know many good men that are working diligently, trying to leave "a piece of change" for their kids, but what can a mom leave for her child when a child asks her this question?

Well, my baby got me thinking; what can I leave her that reflects my love for her? I know that the books that I have written will be a legacy for her to listen to and read, but I wanted to leave her something more than pictures and Facebook videos. I asked God for His direction, and this is what He gave me:

"Journals for Jasmine"

Now, my desire is to create video snippets specifically for my baby girl. I had actually been doing something similar for my niece. Once a week, I will grab my phone and text her a video entitled, "Hi, Baby Sandra!" I would proceed to blow her kisses, show her a lizard, or spell a word for her. Most times, the videos were comical, but what was important is that, since we lived thousands of miles apart, I just wanted to be sure my niece would remember me while she was growing up. It is now my plan to use this same method to leave a legacy of love for my youngest.

"Hi, Jasmine. This is your mom."

This is the way I think I will begin each video. I will record myself putting on makeup or selecting a new wig to wear for the day. How about sending her a video while I am burning dinner (that will instill great memories), or when I am praying to God… won't that be something? I can send her videos of my memories of her as a baby or just a video with me resting on the coconut-scented pillow that she gave me for my birthday. Each video will be specific to her alone, and it will help to remind her of family history, provide tips for "adult-ing," and make suggestions for raising her family. I thank God for this inspiration, and I hope it encourages each of you to leave a specific inheritance of love for your children's children!

- Ask God to instruct you on how to leave a legacy for YOUR children.

- Write the vision; make it plain – (Habakkuk 2:2 KJV) teaches us to write down what God has given us. Try to journal or write down letters to your children!

We all create vision boards for workplace inspiration or personal guidance, so why not make a vision board for your family to pass along to one another?

You know what? I think I like this idea better than leaving money or material possessions for our children. Does leaving a car for a child make them respect the gift or the giver? Does it make them appreciate the hard work you put in to leave them this house, or does it make them understand the scripture any more clearly? I want my children and grandchildren to trust in and follow the scripture that says, *Look at the birds of the air; they do not sow or reap or store away in barns, and yet your heavenly Father feeds them. Are you not much more valuable than they?* (Matthew 6:26 NIV)

Use That Cash-Money

While my daughters were growing up, I was struggling with bad credit. In fact, my credit was so bad that I eventually filed for bankruptcy. With poor credit and a trifling ex-husband that did not want to keep a job, I spent a lot of my time trying to make ends meet. I robbed from Peter to pay Paul, and I taught my daughters how to do the same. I would make a payment arrangement with the electric company in order to pay off the gas company.

I would pay the smallest amount that I could on the phone bill and head to the food bank to get groceries for us all. When we found ourselves homeless and living in extended stay hotels throughout Orlando, I found myself teaching my daughters how to pinch a penny and hold that "cash-money" until the last moment! I never taught my daughters the importance of establishing credit, using it, and keeping it intact.

"Mom, are you going to be home tonight?" my daughter asked as I answered the phone. She even dispensed with the usual pleasantries as I answered the phone and went straight to her question. "Sure, baby, I think I will be home. What time are you talking about?" After we coordinated the details, I headed on my way with my plans, and I wondered why my youngest was driving an hour from

Jacksonville to Daytona Beach Florida to spend the night with me.

"Lord, I'm asking you to look out for my baby girl. I don't know if she is ok or not, but I know that she is in your hands."

"Mom, come out to the car and help me bring my suitcases in the house." *What suitcases (plural)? It is 10 pm, and you said you are leaving in the morning to get to work on time at 10 am, so why do you need help bringing your suitcase(s) in the house?* Even though these questions were floating around in my head, I obediently followed my youngest to the front door and out to the driveway where I immediately saw a new car parked in the driveway.

When you do not teach your children the importance of credit, they have to learn on their own. Fortunately, my children did not fall into the pit of bad credit as I had done; they just learned to pay cash for everything. Therefore, when my youngest was ready to trade in her old used car after patching it back up for the past five years, she found herself frustrated with the lack of finance offers. "You have no credit," was the reply she continued to hear. "How am I supposed to GET any credit if somebody doesn't GIVE me any credit?" was her frustrated response.

Teach your children the importance of saving, living below their means, and establishing GOOD credit. Talk to them early in life about the bills that you pay. This helps them build an appreciation for money; the money you earn, the money you spend on them, and the money they will one day earn for themselves. If you do not know HOW to teach them these tools, take them to a financial planner, a banker, or ask a relative that HAS money to teach you and your child. Do not just tell your child to "save your money," show them HOW to save! My mother saved and cashed in pop bottles as I grew up in Detroit, and she would let me keep half of the money from the bottles that I brought home. I was able to save that money in my savings account in the bank, and I got excited watching the interest make it grow. My dad sat me down and taught me how to read a bill and write the check to pay it. Unfortunately, I missed the lesson on balancing the checkbook BEFORE you wrote the check (lol).

If you do not take this advice from a real mom, you will be paying for their toys, their tuition, their babies, and their cars and houses well into their adult years.

How do you teach your child about money and credit?

_____

_____

_____

How young do you think your children should be BEFORE you start teaching them about money and credit?

_____

_____

_____

What financial mistakes have you made that you want your children to avoid?

_____

_____

_____

How do you feel about co-signing for your child's new car, apartment or furniture?

_____

_____

_____

The Time Is Now 1:38

BY EVANGELIST ANGIE BEE

I was driving down the road. Which road I was driving on, I do not quite remember because I was listening to my GPS tell me which lane to get in and which way to turn. You see, I was driving from Apopka, Florida, to Windermere, Florida, and was struggling to arrive on time for my 2:00 p.m. appointment. Although I had lived in Orlando, Florida, for the majority of my adult life, I needed help navigating this road, and my GPS was screaming at me loudly.

"In 30 feet, merge onto the left two lanes and turn left."

"In 15 feet, turn your steering wheel slightly to the left and merge onto the left two lanes."

"Check your blind spot, turn down the radio so you can hear me and stop chomping so loudly on those chips!"

"Pay attention; you are about to miss your turn!"

Now, that last command from the GPS really got me focused because as I was obediently checking my blind spot in order to merge into the left turn lane, I immediately saw a billboard that read "1:38." That was all that it said; the sign read *1:38*. As I entered the left turn lane and waited for the light to change, I tried to figure out what the sign meant. Did it mean Genesis 1:38? Did it mean Exodus 1:38? I started to try to redirect my mind to scripture references in order to find out what that scripture meant, and I was just about to pick up my phone and ask GOOGLE to look up the scripture for me when my GPS screamed at me again.

"Put down that phone and merge into the right lane. You are gonna be LATE!"

Oh yeah, that is right! Thanks for reminding me that I have a 2:00 p.m. meeting. Thanks for also reminding me that I could get a ticket for playing with my phone while driving.

God has had me on a path lately to check on the "widows" in my life. He even led me to share this word recently with the attendees of a women's empowerment conference where I spoke. The Bible teaches us in 1 Timothy 5:3 to, *Give proper recognition to those widows who are really in need* (NIV). So, in my mind, this means to call them and visit them and listen to them and love them. Currently, I have three grandmothers that are widows and two very dear friends that are widows. Since August 2013, I have lived in Daytona Beach with my anointed husband, so once a month I take a day trip to the Orlando area to visit my two widow friends.

The first widow friend in my life lives in Apopka, Florida, and is now in the beginning stages of some form of mental degradation. She really has been a widow for the twenty-plus years that I have known her, but she was not your average widow! This perky blessing in my life was a godmother to my children, an advisor for my tax returns, and a business partner as we sold makeup together. She always had a lovely story to share with us, and it was a fight to pay our own bill that the waiter brought us after a meal. This widow was the one that advised me to go to the domestic violence shelter towards the end of my last marriage, and this widow has a smile and disposition that will light up a room! Currently, she lives in assisted living with her aged doggie, and I had arrived in time to share chocolate chip cookies with her while sitting in the community room.

"How are the girls?" she asked, referring to my daughters.

"They are fine! They are grown-ups now with jobs and cars and boyfriends," was my exuberant response.

"Oh, that's wonderful! Please give them my love!" she said through the brightest smile.

Just then, the cookies were delivered to our table, and another family arrived in the community area, pushing a stroller that transported an adorable baby. My widow friend and I cooed over the baby as the adults waited patiently for the infant's grandmother to arrive to meet them. We talked about how quickly babies grow up and how we should cherish these days, and we offered the family some of our cookies. The family complimented me on my dress, I thanked them and gave God praise for my garment, and then my widow friend's attention was back in my direction.

"Oh, Angela! Your dress IS lovely, and your skin is just glowing!" she said.

"Thank you so much!" I replied with a blush. "Sometimes you gotta let the sun kiss your face to get this kinda glow on your cheeks!" I beamed. "God is good," I continued and gave my thanks.

"How are the girls?" she asked me again, which was now the third time she asked me this question since my arrival 20 minutes ago (heavy sigh).

But if a widow has children or grandchildren, these should learn first of all to put their religion into practice by caring for their own family and so repaying their parents and grandparents, for this is pleasing to God (1 Timothy 5:4 NIV)

My darling friend has no children. She is thrilled to chat about her nieces, nephews, cousins, and friends, but she has no children, and while my daughters were growing up, this lovely widow loved my girls as if she had birthed them herself.

"Now Jasmine, let me tell you something," she lovingly advised my daughter when she graduated from high school. "When you get to college, and those boys ask you out on a date, tell them "no." Look for a professor to take you on a date. Professors usually have money to pay for the meal!" she said. We all fell out laughing over her humor, and upon reflection, I think Jasmine has never even dated a classmate (she must have taken that advice to heart)! I think about this widow's love quite often, and I pray for her each day.

Another friend and I would jokingly refer to this widow as having the countenance of a nun with her loving gaze and caring expressions. We would even at times compare her face to what we envisioned the wondrous gaze of Mary must have been as she learned that she was to carry the Christ Child.

"See, look at her," we would marvel.

"Look at that joy on her face!"

She almost looked like a child that was seeing something amazing for the very first time.

And Mary said, Behold the handmaid of the Lord; be it unto me according to thy word. Luke 1:38 in the King James Version of the Bible described my blessed friend quite accurately. She is indeed a handmaid of the Lord in the way she has loved on us all, through the years.

And there it was my first scripture reference! Luke 1:38 –

The time is now 1:38.

"Where Are You Staying?"

Have you ever called up a friend or relative and enthusiastically told them that you were coming to their area for a visit, only to hear them respond with, "Where are you staying?" That statement right there lets ME know that I will not be staying with them!

Sometimes it seems as if our door is always open for others, but that hospitality is often not reciprocated. Take for instance an old drinking buddy. You grew up with this fella, and y'all got into much trouble together partying, drinking, drugging, and chasing women together. Then, you both get married, have kids, and move to different areas. Well, whenever HE comes to town to visit, you allow him to stay in your home but when YOU want to come to town for a visit… he asks you, "Where are you staying?"

This scenario reminds me of a dear relative of mine. She is the one that is always sacrificing to purchase helpful gifts and clip coupons for everyone that she knows. She is a giver and can be your biggest cheerleader, too! If you need someone to gossip with, she is right there with you!

If you need a prayer partner, she is calling the intercessory team! She will give her absolutely last and hustle up a solution when you are in need. Unfortunately, when SHE is in need, everyone that she has helped in the past is broke, disgusted, and unavailable for her.

"Where are you staying?"

I began this chapter of the book talking about a billboard sign that I saw as I traveled down a road from one destination to another. My GPS was directing me, and I was daydreaming as I tried to figure out what the sign meant. I was leaving from a visit with one widow and was traveling to meet with another, although at the time of my travels I was not considering her a widow.

You see, my 2:00 p.m.-scheduled meeting was with two very wise women. One was younger than I was and the other was older than I, and I was grateful that they had invited me over. The older woman was a widow. I did not know why they wanted me to visit them, but I have learned that you do not always need to know where you are going, or where you will be staying when you are on the path that the Lord has put you on.

Order my steps in thy word (Psalm 119:133 KJV)

The younger woman that invited me to this meeting is truly a dear friend of mine. She has been in my life for nearly six years now, and we actually met on Facebook! I do not remember how we became connected on social media, but as the result of this friendship, she became our first workshop presenter at the launch of the Moms-n-Ministry workshop in January 2013.

Since that time, we have shared meals, ministry, and

holidays together, and I value the wisdom that she imparts in my life. This friend invited me to the meeting, and I didn't even ask her why.

The second woman that wanted to meet with me is a bodacious, beautiful blessed senior citizen that I have followed on social media for quite some time. I had the pleasure of meeting her professionally and officially at a high school graduation celebration, and just a few months ago, we were both at the same author event in Daytona Beach! Just gazing at her puts a smile on my face, and I feel like I could sit at her feet to relish her stories for hours. I was driving to her home to meet with them both, and I could not wait to get there!

Do you know that Jesus had followers? Yep! Yep! Not just disciples that traveled with him, but followers that kinda stalked Our Lord as well. In the book of John 1:38, quoted from the New International Version it tells us, *Turning around, Jesus saw them following and asked, "What do you want?" They said, "Rabbi" (which means "Teacher"), "where are you staying?*

Jesus had stalkers, and they wanted to know where He was staying. I do not believe any of those inquiring minds were offering Our Lord a place to stay or even a meal, but they wanted to know what his plans were. I envision that they wanted to spend the night with Our Lord and sit at his feet to relish his stories.

I can imagine that! I want to sit at the feet of the older woman that I was driving to see, and I can imagine following her down the road just like those folks that were following Jesus. Those stalkers wanted to spend time with Our Lord, and I can truly understand that feeling.

And there it was; my second scripture reference! John 1:38 –

The time is now 1:38.

"Why Are You Here?"

*"Do you know where you're going to?
Do you like the things that life is showing you? Where are you going to, do you know?"*

These are the lyrics from the theme from *Mahogany*, as sung by Diana Ross; according to Google. Now I must admit I have NEVER seen the movie *Mahogany*. Was it a movie? Is that the movie where Billy D. Williams says to Diana Ross, "Do you want my hand to fall off?"

On the other hand, was that his line from the movie *Lady Sings the Blues*? In any case, I have not seen EITHER of those movies (for shame, for shame), but I do realize that Diana Ross and Billy D. Williams were the power couple of their day!

If you let the Lord guide you in every aspect of your life, you do not really need to know where you are going. You do not even need to know WHY you are going to that destination! All you need to do is follow the path HE has put you on. Think about my obnoxious GPS reference at the beginning of this chapter; I did not know what road my GPS was directing me to take; I was just following the voice commands. You need to feel the same way about the voice of God when He directs you.

Let me give you an example: As I sat down to write this chapter, I knew what my scripture reference was going to be, and I knew that I wanted to complete this chapter before my husband completed his nightly snoring ritual (God bless him!). However, I did not know how I wanted to begin the chapter. I started with the title of this chapter, which was inspired by the scripture, and then I started hearing Diana Ross singing that song in my head, "Do You Know Where You're Going To..." I did not even know the lyrics to the song, so I Googled it. The song's lyrics popped up, and I immediately fell in love with them! I started researching aspects of the movie and realized that I had never seen it. I checked out images of that FINE BLACK MAN Billy D. Williams and realized other movies that I have never seen and got lost in Google for about 30 minutes! That is when the song started playing in my head again.

You see, sometimes it is that still small voice in your head that can put you on the right path. That voice can help you write the best sermon or complete that research assignment. That voice can remind you to stop daydreaming or clicking Google links or to get off Facebook in order to get you back on track, on the right path. Once the song started playing in my head again, I got to work on this chapter!

Do you know where you're going to?

Now remember, I was headed to a meeting with two wise women. I did not know what street I needed to take to get me from point A to point B, but I was listening to the voice of my GPS to direct me. Listen to the voice of the Holy Spirit to guide you. As you are reading this, you probably hear something in your head right now! *Don't you?*

Do you like the things that life is showing you?

Sometimes you will be on a path, and you do not like what you see. You do not like the traffic; you may ignore the panhandlers that you pass by, and you do not like the gas prices that are screaming at your empty gas tank, but you realize that this is life, and it is showing itself to you. Sometimes you are in a situation that you do not know how to get out of, or you want a promotion or a new client. Do you like the things about this life that you see? If you do, you are on a wonderful path, and if you do not, it is time to ask God for guidance.

Where are you going to, do you know?

Now, I knew WHERE I was going to, but I did not know why I was invited. The two wise women invited me to meet with them, but I did not know why they wanted me. I only knew that I needed to be on time for my 2:00 p.m. meeting with them, and I was listening to my GPS give me directions. I was also praying while I was driving. Not only was I praying for the other drivers on the road, but I was praying for God's guidance during the meeting. How would I respond to their topics of discussion? Could I be helpful to them if they needed my assistance? Would they have lunch ready because my belly was growling? You can always have a conversation with God on the way to your destination!

Jesus replied, *Let us go somewhere else—to the nearby villages—so I can preach there also. That is why I have come.* (Mark 1:38 NIV)

That is why I have come. I think that is the most significant line in that verse because it gives you a reason why Jesus was on that path! Why are you on that road that you are? Why are you completing this homework assignment? Why are you still at that job? Why are you going to THAT church or dating THAT man? Why are you ignoring your children or wearing THAT suit? Why are your pants hanging down, and why is your cleavage showing? Is that the reason you have come? I may not have known the reason why the wise women invited me over, but I knew that I was on a path that God had placed me, and I was going to get there ON TIME!

And there it was; my third scripture reference - Mark 1:38

The time is now 1:38

"What Time is it?"

"Father God, I thank you for the words that you have given me to write this book. I ask that this project meet with the eyes and ears of your children that need to hear it, and that they feel compelled to share it. I thank you for the pathways that will lead us to our destination, whether we know where or why. Keep us from hurt, harm or danger, and let our lives be an example for our children and communities. Make me a better daughter, sister, wife, and mother as I strive to be used by you. In the mighty name of Jesus, Amen."

Sometimes, it is time to change direction. It is ALWAYS time to pray, and sometimes that prayer can re-direct you. Consider an entrepreneur that changes the mission of their company after a few years of growth. My company began years ago offering promotional tools for businesses and ministries, and now we produce audio books for authors! We changed our mission. Consider a road-widening project to accommodate a new housing development or even when a student changes their major during their senior year! That is a change in direction as the detours of life move you around to a new pathway. I needed to begin this section with a prayer, and I may end this book with another prayer; let us see what the Lord says for me to do!

My scripture references throughout this book have been based on the first chapter and the thirty-eighth verse from the New International Version of the Bible, and I was able to retrieve those verses from Google. As I was driving down a road headed to a 2:00 p.m. meeting, I saw a billboard that informed me of Chapter 1 and verse 38. I was certain that the billboard was an inspirational message to guide me to a blessed lesson from the Holy Scriptures, and I could not wait for my meeting to end so that I could look up the scripture. Wow! Thank you, God, for your word! I cannot wait to soak it up and bury it deep in my heart!

I arrived at the home of the wise women, and they greeted me with love. I received a tour of the home and was offered a beverage and a slice of one of TWO delicious-looking homemade cakes. We complimented one another with love. Everything was going great, and then the eldest of the wise women said to me, "So, do you know why you are here?"

You do not need to know WHY you are on a path that God has placed you on. All you need to do is follow HIS directions and get there on time. I arrived at the home on time, right at 2:00 p.m. Yes, they fed me lunch, and the plan of God that unfolded during that meeting was truly a blessing! The result of that meeting will be an exciting journey of love, outreach, and giving to our families and our communities, and I can't WAIT to experience it all and share it with each of you.

You do not even need to understand HOW the path that God has placed you on will be given to you. Consider students that attend the school they are zoned for in their community. Consider a song that pops into your head from a movie you have never seen. Now, consider a billboard that leads you to scriptures 1:38 on a road that you cannot even remember driving on.

I now realize that the billboard that I saw that led me to these scriptures AND the composition of this book was not even a billboard at all. The "billboard" was a clock that told me the time of day. It was 1:38 p.m., and I saw that clock on my way to my 2:00 p.m. meeting.

The time is now 1:38.

Thank you, God. I love you.

Hi!

Thank you for purchasing *MAAA!*

Please share these words of love with others as we evangelize together, and know that you are loved and appreciated by me...

"Da QueenBee" Angie BEE

Other Books by Angie BEE

Last Week...I Wanted to Die

Evolution of Da Queen Bee: Praising God for 3 Years of Weight Loss, Healing, Blessing and Service

In the Beginning: There Was God, Me & You (Written with Bartee)

Daily Dose of Direction for Women in Business: A 90 Day Journey to Direct and Guide Women in Business to Succeed (Daily Dose Series) – (Contributing Author)

Evangelist Angie BEE is the founder of *The TOUR that Angie BEE Presents* and the recipient of numerous awards. To book Evangelist Angie BEE or a TOUR event, contact her using one of these methods:

Evangelist Angie BEE
P.O. Box 730073

Ormond Beach, FL 32173
Phone: 407-914-6519
Email: EvangelistAngieBEE@gmail.com
Website: www.DaQueenBEE.com

NOTES

NOTES

NOTES

www.ingramcontent.com/pod-product-compliance
Lightning Source LLC
Chambersburg PA
CBHW052208110526
44591CB00012B/2134

*9 7 8 1 9 4 6 9 8 1 1 4 1 *